GET LUCKY

www.transworldbooks.co.uk

GET *Lucky*

RITUALS, HABITS AND SUPERSTITIONS
OF THE RICH AND FAMOUS

Chas Newkey-Burden

BANTAM PRESS

LONDON · TORONTO · SYDNEY · AUCKLAND · JOHANNESBURG

TRANSWORLD PUBLISHERS
61–63 Uxbridge Road, London W5 5SA
A Random House Group Company
www.transworldbooks.co.uk

First published in Great Britain
in 2014 by Bantam Press
an imprint of Transworld Publishers

A CIP catalogue record for this book
is available from the British Library.

ISBN 9780593073438

Addresses for Random House Group Ltd companies outside the UK
can be found at: www.randomhouse.co.uk
The Random House Group Ltd Reg. No. 954009

The Random House Group Limited supports the Forest Stewardship Council® (FSC®),
the leading international forest-certification organisation. Our books
carrying the FSC label are printed on FSC®-certified paper. FSC is the only
forest-certification scheme supported by the leading environmental organisations,
including Greenpeace. Our paper procurement policy can be found at
www.randomhouse.co.uk/environment

Typeset in Serifa
Printed and bound in Great Britain by Clays Ltd, St Ives plc

2 4 6 8 10 9 7 5 3 1

MIX
Paper from
responsible sources
FSC® C016897

Introduction

The purpose of this book is to entertain, inform and inspire. It is packed with tips that are motivating, thought-provoking and, in some cases, downright eccentric.

In the pages that follow, you will discover the tricks and quirks of some of history's most accomplished and revered figures, including Audrey Hepburn, Winston Churchill, Steve Jobs, Maya Angelou and Charles Dickens.

You will find out, too, which leading crime novelist scribbled his way to international fame while lying down with a martini; which globally bestselling author hangs upside down for inspiration; and the identity of the leading philosopher who used the naked back of his lover as a writing desk.

Read about the novelist who would drink a heart-thumping fifty cups of coffee in a day; the screenwriter who secretly records his family's conversations for inspiration; and the sportsman who concluded that urinating over his own hands was the route to success.

So if you want to know how Franklin Delano Roosevelt rose to the top job in American politics, how Sir Richard Branson became a multi-billionaire or how Marilyn Monroe always looked so glamorous, you have come to the right place. This is a feast of top tips from the rich and famous.

Many of us have compiled a fantasy line-up for a dinner party of famous guests. As our imagination races, we conjure up raucous evenings, in which iconic figures regale us with their charm and anecdotes as the wine flows.

Yet which among us would be able to resist asking our famous guests for just one nugget of advice? Well, in *Get Lucky* you can read such nuggets from one hundred celebrated figures from the past and present.

Lucky you …

Chas Newkey-Burden, summer 2014

WEE ON YOUR HANDS

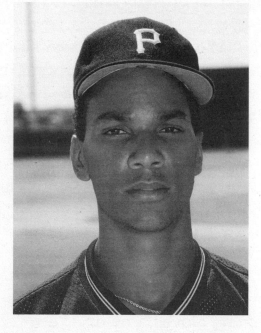

Moises Alou played 1,942 games during his seventeen-season career in Major League Baseball. During his playing years he represented a number of sides, including the Pittsburgh Pirates, the Chicago Cubs and the New York Mets.

WHY MOISES LET IT ALL FLOW

You might be surprised to learn how many sportsmen have pee-centred rituals. Look at Sergio Goycochea (page 82) and Lyoto Machida (page 120). Baseball player Moises Alou took to urinating over his own hands as a success technique during his seventeen years in the National League. The Dominican-American outfielder explained that he took this strange step to toughen up the skin on his hands and to prevent calluses. This allowed him, he said, to strike the ball without having to use batting gloves. The ritual acquired new disciples, including New York Yankees catcher Jorge Posada, who gushed about the benefits of it. But he added a cautionary note: 'You don't want to shake my hand during spring training.'

TREAT ME MEAN

An author and poet, **Maya Angelou** wrote celebrated works including *I Know Why the Caged Bird Sings* and *On the Pulse of Morning*. She was also a respected civil rights activist and a powerful speaker.

ANGELOU'S HOTEL HOVEL

Maya Angelou hired a hotel room in which she wrote. However, this was not some palatial den of indulgence. Instead, for Angelou, less was more. Describing her writing room as 'mean', she explained that it contained no more furniture than a bed and a washbasin. In the room, she kept two books – a dictionary and a Bible – together with a bottle of sherry and a deck of cards. For her, these surroundings and props were the route to literary productivity. While she kept her writing room as sparse and simple as possible to maintain focus, she kept her home 'very pretty'. She normally arrived at the room around 7 a.m., having woken as early as 5.30 a.m.

DON'T MAKE HIM CROSS

Lance Armstrong won the Tour de France a record seven consecutive times between 1999 and 2005. However, since retiring from the sport, the cancer survivor has admitted to doping and been stripped of those titles.

WHY LANCE WORE A CRUCIFIX

During his cycling career, many spectators and fans assumed that Lance Armstrong was a religious man. This was because of the crucifix that hung low and prominently from his neck as he sprinted, climbed and sweated around the gruelling Tour de France course. He also had a five-foot Spanish painting of the crucifixion hanging on the wall of his Austin mansion. However, Lance was not a 'believer' in any religious sense. Instead, he wore the necklace as a reminder of a fellow cancer patient. This way, as he battled his way through another contest, he could remember his friend's battle with cancer. But then, as we've since discovered, there is a lot about Lance we misunderstood.

BAKER'S RULES

Born in the 1920s, **Russell Baker** was known for his comedic writing and satirical statements. He has written for many newspapers and published several books. His autobiography, *Growing Up*, was published in 1982.

SMELL FLOWERS AND SLEEP NAKED

Russell Baker gave a highly memorable commencement speech to Connecticut College in 1985. He offered his enraptured and amused audience several tips for creating successful, fulfilling and happy lives. Among the gems and rituals he offered were: 'Bend down once in a while and smell a flower' and 'Sleep in the nude'. The Pulitzer Prize-winning writer also advised the young men and women to 'Learn to fear the automobile' but never to 'take your gun to town'. Another of his tips edged into the truly surreal. He advised his audience: 'Don't go around in clothes that talk.' Perhaps the sweetest, and certainly simplest, of all was his final tip: 'Smile.'

BRING IT ON, SAYS BALE

Christian Bale first came to fame at the age of thirteen, in *Empire of the Sun*. He has since starred in the *Batman* series and played Dicky Eklund in *The Fighter*. The English actor has also appeared in *American Hustle.*

WHY CHRISTIAN WALKS UNDER LADDERS

Lots of celebrities are almost crippled by superstitions: avoiding the thirteenth floor of buildings, rushing home if they see a black cat and never walking underneath a ladder, for instance. But actor Christian Bale is different. He likes to positively dare superstition to do its worst. 'I walk under ladders, I do all that stuff. I do it on purpose. I like provoking superstitions,' he once said. Whether this makes the famed *Batman* star superstitious or anti-superstitious is a matter for debate. But having taken his place alongside a galaxy of stars in a succession of acclaimed and profitable movies, Bale seems to be enjoying a fair slice of luck.

BALTHUS'S BACCY

Count Balthus Klossowski, known as **Balthus**, was a distinguished modern artist. Born in Paris in 1908, he died in Switzerland in 2001. An enigmatic and controversial talent, he was a leading figurative painter of the twentieth century.

THE ARTISTIC MAGIC OF A CHEEKY SMOKE

The mysterious artist Balthus believed that smoking was an important aid to the creative process. 'I've always painted while smoking,' he said, claiming to 'intuitively' understand that smoking would double his 'faculty of concentration'. Cigarettes allowed him to be 'entirely within a canvas'. Having a cigarette 'between my lips' conjured 'exquisite moments of contemplation'. Even as he grew older and weaker, the Polish-French modern artist continued to use tobacco as a creative aid. He also liked to meditate in front of the canvas, and his painting day would always begin with a prayer. Between these various rituals, he created some memorable works.

CUP OF COFFEE? DON'T MIND IF I DO

Honoré de Balzac was a leading French novelist and playwright of the nineteenth century. His best-known work was the series of short stories and novels *La Comédie Humaine*, an account of French life in his era.

ACTUALLY, I'LL HAVE FIFTY, IF YOU'D BE SO KIND

When Honoré de Balzac was writing his novels he drank a lot of coffee. When I say he drank a lot of coffee, I mean a *lot* of coffee. When I say a *lot* of coffee, I mean up to fifty cups a day. He not only drank coffee, he chewed it, too. The author was known to chew on coffee beans when he was particularly desperate for a more intense 'hit'. He ended up writing an essay about his obsessive love of the drink, entitled 'The Pleasures and Pains of Coffee'. In it, he described coffee as 'a great power in my life'. He died at the age of fifty-one. The cause? Caffeine poisoning.

CAPTAIN CANS THE CANS

David Beckham spent ten years with Manchester United, during which he won a clutch of trophies, including the 1999 treble. He has also turned out for other sides including Preston North End and Real Madrid. He made over a hundred appearances for England, many as captain.

BECKS AND HIS OCD RITUALS

Former England captain David Beckham admits that he struggles with obsessive compulsive disorder. This has helped push him towards a series of rituals that he felt were necessary to perform. 'I have to have everything in a straight line, or everything has to be in pairs,' he said. The football legend has admitted that he has often rearranged hotel rooms to make 'everything perfect'. He will move all the leaflets and books into a drawer. The former Manchester United star's wife also revealed that Beckham will throw away a can of drink from their fridge rather than tolerate an uneven number. 'He's a weirdo,' said Victoria.

JUSTIN GOES JEWISH

Justin Bieber is one of the most successful
pop acts of the twenty-first century. Discovered
on YouTube, he released his first single in 2009.
Since then he has sold over 15 million albums and
collected over 48 million followers on Twitter. His
personal wealth is estimated at $130 million.

BIEBER TURNS BOYCHICK BACKSTAGE

Although some of his colourful behaviour during 2013 and 2014 might suggest otherwise, pop prince Justin Bieber comes from a very religious background. His mother wanted him to be a prophet and he was reared in a conservative evangelical environment. He prays before every concert. Although he is a Christian, Justin has taken to adding a Jewish prayer to his pre-show routine. This began after he overheard his Jewish manager Scooter Braun and musical director Dan Kanter reciting Judaism's central 'Shema' prayer. Bieber explained that he felt that if the Jewish prayer were something Jesus would have said then he wanted to say it as well. The Canadian's multi-faith approach brought his team closer together.

BUG YOUR FAMILY

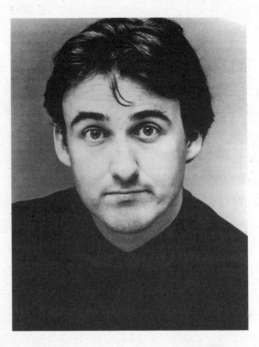

Marc Blake has written a number of sitcoms, several comedy books and three humorous novels. He is also a stand-up comedian and a consultant for sitcom scriptwriters. He has written for comedians including Arnold Brown, Craig Charles, Frankie Howerd and Russ Abbott.

HOW MARC BLAKE UPS HIS DIALOGUE GAME

Scriptwriter and author Marc Blake has found an effective, if mildly sneaky, way of improving his dialogue writing. He found that secretly recording a family meal, then transcribing a few pages of the conversation afterwards, was a great way of noticing the rhythms and quirks of authentic dialogue. 'We need to sculpt dialogue to make it seem real,' he writes in his book *How To Be A Sitcom Writer*, explaining the benefit of this technique. He also acknowledges the naughtiness of his tip, and encourages his readers that once they have learned what they need to from the exercise they must erase the recording, adding: 'You should be ashamed of yourself.'

BLANC'S FRENCH KISS

Laurent Blanc played for several clubs including Napoli, Barcelona and Manchester United. A cultured defender, he won ninety-seven caps for his country, and a World Cup winners' medal in 1998. He has since become a manager of sides including Paris Saint-Germain.

HOW TO PUCKER UP FOR THE WORLD CUP

A kiss is just a kiss – unless it is a puckering ritual that leads to your country winning the football World Cup. French defender Laurent Blanc took to kissing the bald head of a teammate, goalkeeper Fabien Barthez, before each game at the 1998 World Cup finals. It made for quite an arresting sight: the big-haired Blanc kissing the vast, barren orb of Barthez. But Blanc's superstition worked – the French went all the way to the final, in which they beat the mighty Brazil. The French team had another tradition during the tournament: listening to the Gloria Gaynor song 'I Will Survive' in the dressing room.

CHICKEN AT FIRST BASE

Wade Anthony Boggs was born in 1958.
He spent most of his professional career with
the Boston Red Sox. He also turned out for the
New York Yankees and Tampa Bay Devil Rays.
He recorded his three-thousandth hit with the
Devil Rays.

WADE'S FOWL PLAY

Wade Boggs enjoyed an eighteen-year career in professional baseball between the early 1980s and late 1990s. Naturally, during that time, Boggs, and the world around him, changed in so many ways. However, there was one constant: like Jason Terry (page 170), he ate chicken before every single game. The Boston Red Sox third baseman had other superstitions, too. For instance, Boggs woke up at the same time every day, and was fascinated with the number 17. But it was his love of chicken on match days that really captured the public's imagination. Cashing in on the subject, he wrote and published a cookbook about his favourite poultry, called *Fowl Tips: My Favorite Chicken Recipes*.

BORG'S BUSHY BEARD

One of the most iconic players in tennis history,
Björn Borg won eleven Grand Slam singles
titles during his illustrious career. He won five
consecutive Wimbledon titles between 1976 and
1980, and added six French Open singles titles to
his impressive list of honours.

WHY THE SWEDE GREW IT OUT

It's one of the most distinctive and memorable trademarks in tennis history – but Björn Borg's beard was about more than just looking cool. The Swedish tennis legend would always grow his beard before the Wimbledon fortnight. As a secondary superstition, he also wore the same Fila shirt throughout the famous tournament. These quirks of appearance filled him with confidence and gave him the almost icy coolness that became synonymous with his play. Professionals in other sports took notice of his 'lucky beard', and several people in hockey and American football copied him, making it a trend. Some of them went on to win trophies, but it will always be Borg who is the beast of the beard.

BRANSON'S BLACK BOOK

Businessman **Sir Richard Branson** was born in 1950. He is best known as the founder of the Virgin Group, which consists of more than 400 companies. He was knighted in 2000.

RICHARD THE NOTEKEEPER

Richard Branson believes that writing everything down is his most valuable habit. He describes the practice as 'near-obsessive'. He has a black notebook, which he tries to carry everywhere with him. If for some reason the notebook is not available, he will write his notes on the back of his hand. The notes he keeps are varied: they will include ideas that have come to him during the day, notes of meetings he has held, drafts of letters he intends to write, and inspirational quotes he has heard. He will also keep 'diary' style scribblings of his day, like the time he was asked at an airport for his passport, purely because the immigration agent was curious to know his age.

BROWN GOES UPSIDE DOWN

Dan Brown is the author of several novels, the best known of which is *The Da Vinci Code*. Since its publication in 2003, the book has sold over 80 million copies (as of 2014). It has also been adapted into a hit movie. In total, Brown has sold over 200 million copies of his novels.

GET THE BLOOD AND IDEAS RUSHING TO YOUR HEAD

Dan Brown finds that hanging himself upside down helps him to write well. This technique, known as inversion therapy, involves him slipping on a pair of gravity boots and hanging upside down from a specially built frame he has installed in his home. 'You've just got to relax and let go,' he told the *Sunday Times*. 'The more you do it, the more you let go. And then soon it's just, wow.' He has other rituals too. He has an hourglass on his writing desk. At the turn of each hour he stops working and does press-ups or sit-ups. So, as well as writing internationally bestselling novels, Brown must also be in fine physical fettle.

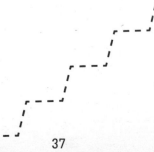

BETTER THAN BUFFETT

Warren Buffett is an American businessman and philanthropist. The chairman and CEO of Berkshire Hathaway, he is consistently ranked as one of the world's wealthiest and most influential individuals. He was born in Nebraska in 1930.

WHY WARREN SEEKS SUPERIORS

Warren Buffett has several criteria for which types of business he will, and will not, invest in. But as well as tips for how to succeed in business, the billionaire has an underlying ritual for success in life. He believes that the trick is to gravitate towards superiors. 'It's better to hang out with people better than you,' said Buffett. 'Pick out associates whose behaviour is better than yours and you'll drift in that direction.' He also says that the very concept of success is about love, rather than lucre. 'When you get to my age, you'll measure your success in life by how many of the people you want to have love you actually do love you,' he says. 'That's the ultimate test of how you've lived your life.'

THE MORNING PAGES

Julia Cameron is an award-winning poet, playwright, screenwriter and filmmaker. A bestselling author, she has written thirty books, including a hard-hitting crime novel *The Dark Room*, children's poetry collections, and her creative guidebook, *The Artist's Way*, which has sold 4 million copies worldwide. She teaches internationally.

A RITUAL TO EVADE YOUR CREATIVE CENSOR

Julia Cameron follows and recommends a daily practice called the 'morning pages' to conjure the creative spirit. Each morning, after she wakes, she writes three pages of stream-of-consciousness longhand writing. She believes this is the 'primary tool of creativity', allowing the artist to leave on the pages 'all that angry, whiny, petty stuff' that 'stands between you and your creativity'. Cameron began the daily practice after her third screen project in a row had been scrapped. Through her morning pages her confidence and creativity returned, and she began to develop a character that formed the basis of a novel she would go on to write. She is now an internationally recognized teacher of creativity as well as a bestselling author.

THE HORIZONTAL HABIT

Born in 1924, **Truman Capote** is the author of more than a dozen works including novels, plays, short stories and novellas. He had decided by the age of eleven that he wanted to write for a living. His best-known texts are the novella *Breakfast at Tiffany's* and the true-crime book *In Cold Blood*.

HOW TO GET PAID FOR LYING DOWN

Each to their own: where Dan Brown goes upside down (page 36), Truman Capote preferred to go horizontal. The crime noir author would lie down to write. He took to writing longhand with a pen in one hand and a drink in the other. Sometimes the beverage would be coffee, on other occasions it would be something a little stronger, like a martini or a sherry. It worked for him. In 1957, he told the *Paris Review*: 'I am a completely horizontal author. I can't think unless I'm lying down, either in bed or stretched on a couch and with a cigarette and coffee handy. I've got to be puffing and sipping.'

CHEEVER'S CHANGEOVER

John Cheever wrote short stories and novels.
He is best known for his shorter works, including
The Enormous Radio and *The Country Husband*.
Some dubbed him 'the Chekhov of the suburbs'.
Born in 1912, he died in 1982.

AN AUTHOR'S SHIFTING CLOTHING

If you saw John Cheever on his way to work each morning during the 1940s, you would never have guessed what clothes he wore as he sat at his writing desk. He would don a smart suit and take the elevator down from his ninth-floor New York apartment. However, rather than alighting at the ground floor as his fellow passengers would, Cheever would carry on down to the basement. He had a makeshift office there. As he arrived, he would remove his suit and write in his underwear until lunchtime. At which point he would dress again and return to his apartment to eat, before taking the rest of the day off.

ONE, TWO, THREE . . .

A leading American business executive,
Kenneth Irvine Chenault was born in the
1950s. He has been the CEO and chairman of
American Express since 2001. He studied at
Harvard Law School before becoming the third
African-American CEO of a Fortune 500 company.

HOW THE AMEX BOSS DEFINES HIS DAY

The CEO of American Express, Kenneth Chenault, likes to hit the ground running in the morning. In order to get going quickly and efficiently, he prepares the night before by writing a simple list of the three top things he wants to accomplish the next day. This trio of tasks is the first thing he looks at each morning. 'Leadership,' he has said, 'is a privilege. If you do not rise to the challenge then you should lose that privilege.' Thanks to his list-keeping tradition, Chenault approaches each day in a focused way. He believes leadership is a quality that can be learned by those willing to listen. And to list, it seems.

THE NAKED TRUTH

Winston Churchill was the British prime minister who led the country to victory against Nazi Germany. He served two reigns as PM, from 1940 to 1945, and 1951 to 1955. **Tony Blair** was the architect of 'New Labour' and served as PM between 1997 and 2007.

MEET WINSTON AND TONY 'BARE'

What do Winston Churchill and Tony Blair have in common? Both have served as prime minister and both oversaw Britain's role in historic wars. However, both men also held meetings naked. Churchill, who kept irregular sleeping patterns, often held War Cabinet meetings in the bath. As spin doctor Alastair Campbell revealed in his diaries, Blair would sometimes summon him to his bathside for an important discussion. In April 1998, an anxious Blair called Campbell to come and chat with him while he was in the bath. It seems Blair was unabashed about being seen naked. On another occasion Campbell arrived at a meeting to find the Labour leader naked, reading the *Daily Mail.*

UNCLE'S UGLY STRIDES

Former Belgian tennis ace **Kim Clijsters** was born in 1983. During her career she won forty-one singles titles and eleven doubles titles. She was often a world number one. She appeared in *Time* magazine's '30 Legends' list.

WHY KIM LOVES GREEN PANTS

Grand Slam tennis champion Kim Clijsters had a ritual which required the cooperation of a relative. It all began when she won the Australian Open in 2011. She thanked her uncle for sparking a new superstition for her. He had worn, she said, 'the ugliest green pants I've ever seen'. She believes that these trousers helped her on her way to victory. 'Those green pants have brought me a little bit of luck,' she said. So, she told her uncle, he would very much be expected to wear them at every match in the future.

HOPPING MAD

Sidonie-Gabrielle Colette, who lived between 1873 and 1954, was a French novelist. She was often known simply as Colette. Her best-known work is the novel *Gigi*, about a young Parisian girl, which was the basis for a 1940s movie.

COLETTE'S FLEA CIRCUS

Colette had a peculiar way of getting warmed up for her writing. She would search her French bulldog Souci's fur for fleas – and pluck any of the little blighters she could find. Colette would also give Souci a good cuddle to get her literary mood flowing. She also had cats and would subject them to a thorough flea-removal session when she was struggling to get the words out. It was not only fleas she hunted – the author would also search for flies in her home and swat any she discovered. Having taken on the hopping fleas and flapping flies, she could settle down to write.

COWELL'S INVISIBLE SIGNS

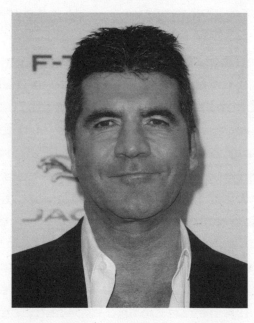

Born in 1959, **Simon Cowell** is a record company executive, talent show judge and television producer. After launching acts including Westlife and Robson & Jerome, Cowell became internationally famous as a straight-talking judge on shows such as *Pop Idol, American Idol* and *X Factor*. Through these shows he has launched the careers of Leona Lewis, Susan Boyle and One Direction. He has an estimated personal fortune of £300 million.

HOW TO SEE THE 'X FACTOR' IN EVERYONE

The ever-ambitious Simon Cowell was taught a charm trick by his father, Eric. Cowell senior, an estate agent and record label executive, told his budding businessman son: 'Imagine that everybody around you has an invisible sign on their head which says "make me important".' It is a trick that Cowell uses to this day. 'What I try and remember is that when I make a show, everyone has played a part in it,' he told CNN. 'The show is created, truthfully, by five hundred people every week.'

CRUYFF'S THUMPING DUTCH COURAGE

One of the most celebrated players in footballing
history, Dutchman **Johan Cruyff** has played
for and managed both Ajax and Barcelona.
Inextricably linked with the 'total football'
philosophy, he was voted European Player
of the Century in 1999.

AND A GUM DEAL FOR JOHAN

Johan Cruyff's rituals seemed bizarre on the face of it. The Dutch footballing legend would always punch his teammate Gert Bals in the stomach before a match began. A slightly less aggressive, but scarcely less peculiar habit of Cruyff's was to spit his chewing gum into the opponent's half of the field just before kick-off. He felt that the influence of this latter habit was vindicated when he forgot his gum in the European Cup Final of 1969. His Ajax side lost 4–1 to AC Milan. Since moving into management, Cruyff has gone all rational on us and urged coaches to discourage superstitious rituals among their players. Well, if that means fewer players thumping their colleagues in the stomach, it can only be a good thing.

ELLEN'S ADVICE?

An American stand-up comedian, television host and actress, **Ellen DeGeneres** starred in the sitcom *Ellen* for several years during the 1990s, before hosting *The Ellen DeGeneres Show*. She has also judged *American Idol* and starred in movies.

DON'T EVER TAKE (OR GIVE) ADVICE

When Ellen DeGeneres spoke at Tulane University in 2009, her advice was slightly bizarre and, in the context, counter-intuitive. She told the students: 'Don't take anyone's advice.' The comedian also told them not to give advice, arguing: 'It will come back and bite you in the ass.' She has, as best she can, lived her message. She feels that never giving or seeking advice allows everyone to live 'with integrity' as an 'honest and compassionate person'. The star of her own US chat show added: 'Never follow anyone else's path, unless you're in the woods and you're lost and you see a path and by all means you should follow that.'

DISCIPLINE –
DEMOSTHENES STYLE

Demosthenes, who lived from 384 to 322 BC, was a renowned statesman of ancient Athens. His celebrated speeches remain a fine document of the politics and lifestyle of ancient Greece. He was acclaimed as the 'perfect orator'.

HOW THE GREEK ORATOR KEPT (HALF) HIS HEAD

Demosthenes felt that focus was vital when he was rehearsing his oratory. He wanted to hone his craft to perfection. To help him remain disciplined and resist the lure of distractions, he would rehearse his speeches in a specially constructed subterranean study. Before going underground, the Greek orator would have the hair on half of his head shaved off. His thinking was that he looked so ridiculous that he would be disinclined to wander off and would instead knuckle down. He would often spend two or three months there practising his oratory, the result of which was widely recognized as a fine thing to witness. It was a bizarre technique – but one that worked.

CHAS'S NORTHWARD KIP

A leading author of the Victorian era, **Charles Dickens** penned some of English literature's most celebrated books and memorable characters. His works include *Oliver Twist, A Tale of Two Cities* and *Great Expectations*. He died in 1870 but his works are as relevant today as ever.

HOW DICKENS ALIGNED WITH THE EARTH'S CURRENTS

Charles Dickens believed that it was important to sleep facing north. To this end, the novelist carried a compass with him so he could adjust the bed wherever he laid his hat. This ritual was based on a belief, which gained currency in the late nineteenth century, that for proper circulation of the blood as you rested it was vital to be aligned with the earth's magnetic field. Dickens' daughter described her father as a 'fidget'. Even if he were staying in a hotel room for just one night, she wrote, he would rearrange the furniture 'to suit the requirements of the electrical currents of the earth'.

NOEL'S WINNING CARDS

Noel Edmonds is a broadcaster whose career took off in the 1970s. He presented *Top of the Pops, Multi-Coloured Swap Shop, Telly Addicts* and *Noel's House Party*, before disappearing from our screens in 1999. He returned in 2005 with *Deal or No Deal*.

HOW TO DEAL (OR NO DEAL) WITH NEGATIVITY

Noel Edmonds is a disciple of positive thinking and cosmic ordering. While the latter belief system might be too 'out there' for the tastes of some, he also has a few down-to-earth rituals. He has written on a small card a list of ten positive words that he feels describe himself. He takes out the list and reads it whenever he feels low, or before a vital meeting or tricky social situation. He also wrote down all his feelings of guilt, anger and sadness on a card, which he then folded into an envelope and burned. He felt this buried the negativity of his past. Given how successfully he resurrected his career, his rituals are worth consideration.

UPPERS PLUS UPPERS . . .

Paul Erdős was born in Budapest, Hungary, in 1913. He inherited his love of mathematics from his parents, who both worked in the field. Working with numerous collaborators, he explored many dimensions of mathematics and is one of the subject's most famous sons.

. . . EQUALS MATHEMATICS GENIUS

'A mathematician,' said Paul Erdős, 'is a machine for turning coffee into theorems.' He spoke from experience: the Hungarian numerical genius ingested plentiful uppers and spewed multiple maths. He would often work nineteen-hour days, such was his commitment to his work. To keep awake during these marathon mathematical missions, the eccentric Erdős would swig Benzedrine and Ritalin down with espresso drinks. He would also neck caffeine tablets. These frenzied habits began following the death of his mother. Friends of the numbers man sometimes urged him to slow down. He always responded the same way: 'There'll be plenty of time to rest in the grave.' He died in 1996, at the age of eighty-three.

A DOUBLE ESPRESS-MO

Mo Farah was born in Mogadishu, Somalia, in 1983. He moved to England at the age of eight and became a renowned runner even as a schoolboy. At the London 2012 Olympics he won two gold medals and has since become a world champion. He was awarded a CBE in the Honours list in 2013.

HOW FARAH STRIKES GOLD

Baristas and barbers do rather well out of Mo Farah. The double-Olympic gold medallist has two particular pre-race quirks that he believes help power him to success. First, he likes to have his head shaved. Mo loves running his hand over the smooth scalp and feeling the invigorating splash of cold water upon it. Then, with around twenty minutes to go before the starting pistol is fired, Farah will be necking coffee, usually in the form of an espresso. Sometimes, he even drinks two. He sank a brace before running in the 10,000 metres at the London 2012 Olympics. He won gold in the race, the first Briton to do so. These men and their caffeine, eh?

TENDER IS THE GIN

One of the most respected American authors of the twentieth century, **F. Scott Fitzgerald** was the author of four completed novels, including *The Great Gatsby.* He was a pivotal part of the 'Lost Generation' of the 1920s.

WHY FITZGERALD FANCIED ITS FLAVOUR

Neat gin – that was a favoured writing fuel of F. Scott Fitzgerald. The celebrated author of *Tender is the Night* said he was often imbibing the famous spirit as he wrote that work. He chose gin out of the range of alcoholic drinks because he believed it brought the effects on fastest and also left less of a telltale smell on his breath. Set on the French Riviera in the 1920s, *Tender is the Night* was his fourth novel. Although gin was central to its creation, Fitzgerald later wondered whether his ritual had been such a good idea after all. He told his editor it had become 'increasingly plain' that the writing and revision of a manuscript 'do not go well with liquor'.

ASSESS YOUR DAY

Often considered the 'First American', **Benjamin Franklin** led an accomplished life as everything from a politician to an author, scientist and inventor. He was born in 1706 and died in 1790. He is remembered for inventions in the electrical field.

BENJAMIN'S FRANK NIGHTLY SELF-EXAMINATION

Benjamin Franklin believed the trick to on-going success was regular self-examination. To do this, he would ask himself the same, simple question every night before he went to bed: 'What good have I done today?' In his quest for what he described as 'moral perfection', the famed inventor paused to assess each day after darkness fell. As well as tidying his mind, he would also tidy his living quarters. Before turning in for the night he would 'put things in their places'. However, it was the tracking of his progress in self-improvement that most stood out in the routine of this revered founding father of the United States.

PJS AT THE PIANO

George Gershwin wrote some of the most memorable compositions of his era, including *Rhapsody in Blue*, *An American in Paris* and the opera *Porgy and Bess*. He also wrote celebrated film scores. He composed several works with his brother Ira. He died in 1937.

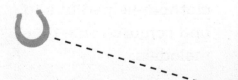

GEORGE GERSHWIN'S COMPOSING CLOTHING

Many office-bound workers view the working existence of the freelance artist as one of blissful, pyjama-clad freedom. In the case of George Gershwin, they are half right. The legendary American composer and pianist was a confirmed workaholic. He compared himself to a boxer, arguing that the successful songwriter must 'always keep in training'. He lived his life accordingly, often working for more than twelve hours a day. However, he typically spent much of his working day perched at his Steinway piano in pyjamas and dressing gown. He would smoke cigars as he tinkled. From his window he had an enviable view of Manhattan. His relaxed clothing helped him to put in the hours and conjure some timeless and memorable melodies.

YOU CAN'T GO THONG

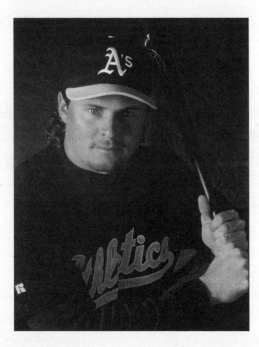

Jason Giambi's career as a first baseman and designated hitter began with the Oakland Athletics before he spent six years with the New York Yankees. He was named one of *Men's Fitness*'s 'Top 10 Most Superstitious Athletes'.

THE BASEBALL SLUGGER WHO WORE GOLD

Burly men wearing gold thongs may not
be your thing but it was very much the
thing of New York Yankees player Jason
Giambi. He wore a gold lamé thong for
matches and found it did the trick if
he was trying to work his way out of a
slump in form. 'It works every time,' he
said. He advised his teammates to try
wearing a similar undergarment. One of
them admitted that he had done so and
it had helped. He put this down less to
mystical powers and more to the fact that
he was concentrating on the discomfort
of the thong rather than getting anxious
about the match. Another teammate
commented: 'Jason is rather strange.'

HOLY WATER IS A GIVEN

Shay Given has kept goal for a host of clubs including Blackburn Rovers, Newcastle United and Aston Villa. He won over a hundred caps for the Republic of Ireland, and appeared at the 2002 World Cup finals.

WHY SHAY PLAYED LIQUID FOOTBALL

Prior to every match he competed in, Irish goalkeeper Shay Given would place a vial of Lourdes holy water at the back of his goal as a lucky charm. 'I carry it in my kitbag and it goes everywhere with me,' he told the *Irish News of the World*. Catholics believe that the special water contains powers linked to the Lourdes spring, where apparitions of the Virgin Mary first appeared in 1858. Given was not the first Irish goalie to take something special to the field. His predecessor in goal for the Republic of Ireland was Paddy Bonner, who would take a piece of clay from County Donegal on to the pitch in his glove bag.

A KID IN A SWEET SHOP

Chris Gorman has been named by no less
an authority than Sir Richard Branson as an
entrepreneur to admire. The co-founder of DX
Communications and the launcher of the Reality
Group, he is also the executive chairman of the
Gadget Shop.

HOW TO BUILD YOUR HOUSING HUNGER

Looking around houses you cannot afford to buy as you wallow in tens of thousands of pounds of debt – how does that sound to you? Frustrating? That is precisely why the entrepreneur Chris Gorman did it. Having built a career as a salesman, Gorman was left with nothing when he was forced to sell his house at a loss. Living in a council house and £30,000 in debt, he decided to go and look at show homes every weekend to reignite his ambition. He compared the experience to offering sweets to a child then taking them away. 'It makes you want it more,' he said. It worked: Chris and his wife are now worth over £45 million.

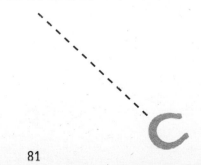

PEE IS FOR PENALTY

Sergio Goycochea played for twelve clubs during his nineteen-year football career. He also made forty-four appearances for the Argentinian national team, and was on the winning side as his nation won the 1993 Copa America. Away from the field he has modelled and appeared on television sports shows.

LETTING GO WHEN YOU'RE PUT ON THE SPOT

For goalkeepers, penalty shoot-outs can be nerve-racking experiences. Back in 1990, Argentinian goalie Sergio Goycochea adopted a luck ritual to ease the tension. It all started when he was 'caught short' before a penalty shoot-out in the World Cup quarter-final against Yugoslavia. Desperate for a pee, he discreetly answered the call of nature on the pitch. His team won the subsequent shoot-out, so he repeated the trick before the next shoot-out, in the semi-final against Italy. Again, the Argentinians were victorious, and Goycochea felt it was no coincidence. From that day on, he always had a crafty pee on the pitch before facing spot kicks. 'It was my lucky charm and I went before every shoot-out,' he said. 'I was very subtle, nobody complained.'

WHEN CHUNDER STRIKES

Glenn Hall, born in 1931, was an ice hockey goaltender who played for the Detroit Red Wings, Chicago Black Hawks and St Louis Blues. He won the Vezina Trophy on three occasions. He was dubbed 'Mr Goalie'.

HALL HURLED HIS WAY TO VICTORY

When Glenn Hall's hockey teammates were preparing for a game there was one sight they hoped for more than all others – Hall throwing his guts up. Hall played for a phenomenal 502 consecutive games between 1955 and 1963. During that run, he would often vomit before a game. In time, he noticed that he seemed to play much better after he had thrown up, so it became a ritual associated with success in his mind and those of his teammates. They even provided a bucket on the bench, in anticipation of a soaking spew from Hall. 'I felt I played better after, I built myself up to a peak,' he said.

KNUT'S NIGHT NOTES

Knut Hamsun published over twenty novels, as well as poems, short stories and plays. The writer, who was born in 1859, was awarded the Nobel Prize in Literature in 1920. His work spans more than seventy years.

SCRIBBLE SECONDS AFTER YOU WAKE

Have you ever been struck with inspiration during your sleep, and wished you had kept a pen and paper next to your bed so you could note it down? Norwegian author Knut Hamsun kept a notebook by his bed, because he felt that the moments after he woke were particularly 'clear-headed' and found him in a usefully 'impressionable' mood. He went a step further than Julia Cameron and her morning pages (page 40): he would not even switch on the light before he began scribbling away his notes as he lay there. 'It has become my habit and I have no difficulty in deciphering my writing in the morning,' he said. Unsurprisingly, the Nobel Prize-winner's work was known for its stream-of-consciousness style.

PUT A MEDAL ON IT!

Kate Hansen has competed as a luger since 2003. She was born in Burbank in California in 1992. She became the youngest junior world champion in 2008 – at the age of fifteen. One television commentator disapproved of her dancing, saying he wished she would do something 'more sports specific'.

HANSEN LOVES TO 'BE' IN THE MOMENT

American luger Kate Hansen loves to warm up for competition by dancing along to a Beyoncé song. During the 2014 Winter Olympics in Sochi, the twenty-one-year-old's 'strictly Beyoncé' warm-up captured the imagination of people around the world. Hansen explained that the music of the soul singer 'gets me fierce and I get stoked'. Although video footage of her dancing went viral on the internet, Hansen was unconcerned. 'I'm completely in my own world and it doesn't matter who's staring, I'm still going to dance,' she said. Many of those who were staring were doing so in admiration anyway. Beyoncé herself shared a video of Hansen on her Facebook page, appending the comment 'Go Kate!' The seal of approval from the queen of soul.

REVIEW YOUR GOALS

Sahar Hashemi is the co-founder of Coffee
Republic and the confectionery brand Skinny
Candy. She has also worked as a lawyer, serving
a writ on controversial miners' leader Arthur
Scargill. She was made an OBE in 2012.

SAHAR'S SIX-MONTHLY RITUAL

The approach of setting goals for business is so widespread that only a masochist would set themselves the herculean goal of trying to discover where it originated. Variations within the tradition are easier to trace. For instance, Sahar Hashemi believes that regular reviews of her goals have allowed her to thrive. 'I think it's important to review goals every six months because everything around you changes and you have to adapt to that,' she said. When she was planning the launch of her UK coffee chain she visited New York and drank in dozens of coffee bars to research the trade. It must have been energizing work.

AND THE WINNER IS . . .

Audrey Hepburn was an icon of the film and fashion worlds. The Brit was born in 1929 and by the 1940s was an established actress. She went on to appear in films including *Breakfast at Tiffany's* and *My Fair Lady*.

. . . HEPBURN'S LUCKY DRESS

Audrey Hepburn was so excited when she was nominated for her first Academy Award. The year was 1954, and she was up for a Best Actress gong for her part in the movie *Roman Holiday*. She chose a dress she had worn on set and asked a renowned designer, Edith Head, to adapt it so she could wear it on the big night. Head made a series of changes, including adjustments to the back and the straps. When Hepburn won the award on the night, she credited her garment, describing it as her 'lucky dress', and wore it again in the future. However, when the floral dress was put up for auction in London that luck seemed to run out – it failed to sell.

HOW TO HANG YOUR RIVAL

Henrik Ibsen was a distinguished playwright, theatre director and poet. Among his many celebrated works are *A Doll's House, An Enemy of the People* and *The Master Builder*. He is credited as being one of the founders of Modernism on the stage.

IBSEN'S INDIRECT TRIBUTE TO AN ENEMY

Playwright Henrik Ibsen found that the best way to motivate himself was to remind himself of his rivals. Ibsen and August Strindberg were described as 'the giants of the theatre of our time' – but there was little love lost between the men. In 1895, Ibsen, the father of realism on the stage, placed a smouldering portrait of his arch-enemy above his writing desk, dubbing it 'the madness incipient'. He wrote: 'He is my mortal enemy, and shall hang there and watch while I write.' Strindberg was not known for his warmth or friendliness. But his brooding presence above Ibsen's desk seemed to work wonders for the nineteenth-century Norwegian's own output.

INCE'S SHIRTY TARRY

Born in 1967, **Paul Ince** was midfield general
for several sides including West Ham United,
Manchester United and Inter Milan. He also won
over fifty caps for England. After retiring he tried
his hand at management.

WHY THE 'GUVNOR' PUT IT ON LATE

When it comes to most sporting pursuits,
everyone wants to finish first. However,
many footballers make an effort to come
on to the pitch last. Paul Ince, that
mainstay of the Manchester United
and England midfields during the 1990s,
had a superstition that made him always
want to put his shirt on last and emerge
on to the field last. Ince's habit of putting
his shirt on late came from common sense
rather than superstition. He would get
very hot during the pre-match warm-up
and during the subsequent psyching up in
the changing room. The first time he left
his shirt off until the last moment, his side
won 5–0. So he stuck with it.

KEEPING QUIET

David James MBE began his career with
Watford in the 1980s. During the following
decade, as a Liverpool player, he also represented
England on fifty-three occasions. One of the
beautiful game's celebrated pin-ups, he has
worked as a model for Giorgio Armani and as a
television pundit.

SPIT AT THE WALL TO KEEP YOUR SHEET CLEAN

Many footballers have 'obsessive' routines that go 'way beyond the normal', says former Liverpool and England goalkeeper David James. He's absolutely right. Take James himself, for instance. His elaborate rituals, which he described as 'mental machinery', began the evening before each game. He would not speak to anyone and he would seek out a urinal, wait until it was deserted then spit against the wall. Eccentric stuff, but he believed it made a difference to his performance between the sticks. 'I was in this mad little world where as long as I did everything in the right order then anything could be achieved,' he wrote later. As we can see, many of his fellow professionals do indeed have rituals that go far beyond the normal.

JOBS' JUMPERS

Steve Jobs (1955–2011) was the co-founder
of Apple Inc. An entrepreneur, marketer and
inventor, he is one of the men most associated
and credited with the modern technology
revolution. He has been described as 'the
master evangelist of the digital age'.

HOW TO FREE YOUR MORNING MIND

The photographs of Steve Jobs in a black turtleneck jumper are among the most memorable images of the Apple genius. It is no coincidence at all that so many photographs of him attired this way are in existence. He actually had a collection of a hundred of the sweaters, which he had specially designed for him by the Japanese fashion figure Issey Miyake. Jobs wore one of the hundred identical jumpers every day, freeing his mind up to focus on bigger decisions. Jobs once showed his collection to a writer. 'That's what I wear,' he told him. Eerily, he added: 'I have enough to last for the rest of my life.'

THE RULE OF FIVE

The broadcaster **Tom Keene** is editor-at-large for Bloomberg News and host of *Bloomberg Surveillance* on both Bloomberg Radio and Bloomberg Television. The tireless Tom, who was born in 1952, is also a widely read columnist and blogger.

WHY YOU SHOULD READ AND READ AND READ . . .

Tom Keene believes that the best way to set yourself aside from – and ahead of – the crowd, is to read five books on any topic you want to understand. 'Get past the one book and on to the next topic habit,' he advises. Former Israeli prime minister Menachem Begin was another man who swore by the virtues of heavy reading. 'It is terribly important for an educated man, if he wants to know things, to read a minimum of 150 pages a day,' he believed. Among other advocates of regular reading is sports and financial writer Jonah Keri. His advice to writers? 'Read a lot. Like, A LOT.'

AN OPEN AND SHUT CASE

Stephen King is a leading author of horror, sci-fi and fantasy novels. He has published over fifty books which, between them, have sold more than 350 million copies. Several of his stories, including *The Shining* and *It*, have been adapted for the big screen.

HOW STEPHEN KING WORKS HIS MAGIC

For bestselling author Stephen King, the trick to spinning a gripping yarn lies at the doorway to his study. The author of such works as *Salem's Lot* and *The Shining* always writes with the door closed, then edits his work with the door open. The theory behind this is that the writing process is private, whereas the editing stage is when the author is preparing to surrender his work to the world. King also maintains a fixed routine, starting the writing day between 8 a.m. and 8.30. He believes this consistency allows him to enter a 'creative sleep' at his desk. He aims to write two thousand words per day.

FANGS FOR THE MEMORY

Heidi Klum is a model, designer and actress. She is also a television star, a road she embarked on with her role in the reality television show *Project Runway*. Born in 1973, she was married to the pop star Seal for several years.

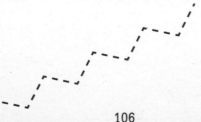

THE FASHION GURU'S BABY TEETH

Model and designer Heidi Klum says that she prefers not to advertise her lucky charm – but she has revealed it to one interviewer. It is indeed a curious one: she carries a bag containing her baby teeth. Once, when she was on a flight, she dropped the bag and had to search for it. A member of the cabin staff came over to ask her what she had lost. 'Yeah, I'm just looking for my teeth,' Klum told him. 'Oh,' replied the flight attendant. Klum had previously tried a more conventional luck-giver: she made a four-leafed clover the emblem of a fashion collection. However, that proved an unlucky charm, as the collection was unusually problematic. Stick with the teeth, Heidi.

LEYVA'S LUCKY TOWEL

Cuban-American gymnast **Danell Leyva** won
bronze at the 2012 London Olympics. He was
already a US national all-around gold medallist
and 2011 world champion. Leyva is a specialist
on the parallel bars and horizontal bar.

THE CLOTH WITH A CULT FOLLOWING

How do you focus when you are facing a big challenge? The American gymnast Danell Leyva drapes the same towel over his head between his exercises. This helps him maintain his concentration. But why always the same towel? He explains that in 2007, two of his aunts presented him with identical towels to use during his sport. He decided that this coincidence was highly symbolic and declared them 'lucky towels'. One of them was torn within months, leaving him with just the one lucky towel. 'It hasn't left my side ever since,' he told Yahoo! The towel has developed something of a cult following, and even has its own Twitter account: @LeyvasTowel.

GARY'S GOAL PRESERVATION

After beginning his career with Leicester City in 1978, **Gary Lineker** appeared for Everton, Barcelona, Tottenham Hotspur and Nagoya Grampus Eight. He is the second highest all-time goal-scorer for England. Now a top sports broadcaster, he was awarded an OBE in 1992.

KNOWING WHEN NOT TO SHOOT

Gary Lineker seemed like a goal machine during his successful footballing career. He scored 192 league goals and another 48 for England. However, football's Mr Nice Guy would never take a shot at goal during the pre-match warm-up. He did not want to 'waste' a goal, so while other strikers will unleash a torrent of shots during the warm-up, Lineker preferred to keep his powder dry until the match officially kicked off. If he had failed to score in the first half of a match, he would change his shirt during the interval. On the rare occasions that he went on a prolonged goalless run, he would get his hair cut to try to end the goal drought.

 - - - - - - - - - -

LYNCHES WHO LUNCH

The renowned film and television director **David Lynch** was born in 1946. He is known for his surrealist style, in television series such as *Twin Peaks* and body horror films like *The Elephant Man* and *Eraserhead*.

DAVID'S DELICIOUS DATES

Back in the 1980s, filmmaker David Lynch swore by sugar. For seven years of his life, he would eat lunch at the same eatery: the evocatively titled Bob's Big Boy. He would arrive after the main lunchtime diners had left, and consume a highly sugary chocolate milkshake followed by several cups of very sugary coffee. You will not be surprised to learn that this sugar fest gave him quite a 'rush'. A rush from which, he said, he would 'get so many ideas!' As the ideas flowed, he wrote them down on napkins at his table. If he had forgotten to bring a pen, a waitress would lend him one on the proviso that he'd return it before he left the restaurant. Well, it seems a reasonable deal.

WHITE RABBITS!

James McAvoy began his acting career on television when he was still in his teens. The Scot then moved on to stage and into films. He has appeared in *Atonement*, *The Chronicles of Narnia* and the *X-Men* series and the comedy-drama *Filth*.

A SAYING OF LUCK AND PROTECTION

If you ever meet the actor James McAvoy on the first day of the month, you can expect one thing: he may well say the words 'white rabbits' to you. The star of *Filth* says he learned this tradition from his grandmother. She taught him that it is good luck to utter the saying to the first person he sees on the first day of every month. The Scottish actor is not alone in this. A number of people do it. During the Second World War, RAF aircrew believed that saying 'white rabbits' the moment they awoke in the morning would protect them during the battles and horrors to come.

McCAIN'S MYTHOLOGY

John McCain was born in 1936. He served in the US navy and was shot down and taken hostage during the Vietnam War. He entered politics in the 1980s and ran for US presidency in 2008.

THE RITUALISTIC RIGHT-WINGER

Obama's electoral opponent in the 2008 presidential elections was John McCain. The Republican veteran is one of American politics' most superstitious figures. He has a clutch of good-luck possessions, including a feather, a pen and a blue jumper. Other fortune-favouring items he keeps include a compass, a pair of lucky shoes and a lucky penny. There's more: he wears a lucky rubber band, visits a lucky hotel room and even has a lucky town – Peterborough in New Hampshire. On election nights, he likes to watch a film as the results begin to materialize. Sitting next to him, his wife Cindy will be dressed in a purple outfit, which she believes helps bring luck. None of this brought much fortune to McCain at the 2008 polls, of course.

SOME RED-HOT TIPS

Footballer **Archibald Renwick Macaulay** began his career with Rangers, winning a cup and league medal. In 1937 he moved to London, turning out for West Ham United, Brentford and Arsenal. He later managed several sides, including West Bromwich Albion.

HOW EIGHT CIGGIES USED TO HELP YOU WIN

An insight into how much the game of football has changed over the years can be found by examining the training rituals of players from long-gone eras. For instance, Arsenal's wing-half Archie Macaulay was asked during the 1947/48 season for his tips on healthy eating and living. 'During training I limit myself to eight cigarettes daily and keep off intoxicants,' he replied. In the football of the 1940s, smoking eight cigarettes a day might have given you the edge as an Arsenal player. The Gunners won the title the year of Macaulay's interview. Nowadays, under the healthy regime installed by Frenchman Arsène Wenger, it would probably leave you choking as your opponents merrily ran rings around you.

TAKING THE . . .

Mixed martial arts fighter **Lyoto Machida** was born in Brazil in 1978. He began fighting in his teens and was a black belt at the age of thirteen. He competes as a middleweight and is a former UFC Light Heavyweight Champion.

MACHIDA'S NUMBER-ONE BEVERAGE

Laughter is the best medicine, or so they say. Lyoto Machida disagrees. He believes that urine is the best medicine. The martial arts champion began a strange habit after his father advised him it would be beneficial. 'I drink my urine every morning like a natural medicine,' Machida told Brazilian magazine *Tatame*. He accepts that it is a bizarre practice and found that people assumed he was joking when he revealed it. Experts say that urine contains hormones, minerals and other elements that help meld moisture to protein. Machida's father, Yoshizo, claims that it helps flush the system clean. He compares it, in its benefits, to a vaccine.

KISSING THE BALL

Lashit Malinga was a fast bowler for the Sri Lankan national side. He set several records, including for both the speed of his deliveries and the number of batsmen they dispatched. Born in 1983, he retired from test cricket in 2011.

MALINGA'S MANY MWAHS

Lashit Malinga developed a ritual of kissing the cricket ball before he bowled it. This led to him giving it a succession of smackers during a long day's cricket, but for him the relentless smooching was well worth it. Over his career he must have kissed more balls than you have had hot dinners. When a cricket fan suggested to Malinga that kissing before each run-up was taking the ritual too far, Malinga was unrepentant. 'Cricket is my job and my livelihood,' explained the Sri Lankan. 'As a result, being a bowler, I have the greatest respect for the cricket ball and I've got into the habit of kissing it before I start my run-up.'

PSALM LIKE IT HOT

Curtis Martin competed in the National Football League for the New England Patriots and New York Jets over a ten-year career. Martin retired in 1998. He was installed in the Pro Football Hall of Fame in 2012.

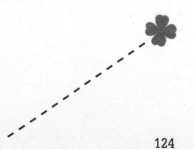

MARTIN'S MAIN MANTRA

American football is not a game for the faint-hearted. Yet the former New York Jets running back Curtis Martin prepared for battle by reading a biblical passage. The star read Psalm 91 before each game. Known informally by some as the 'Psalm of protection', the passage speaks of how the Lord, who serves as a 'refuge' and 'fortress', will save the holy from 'the fowler's snare and from deadly pestilence'. Martin would read of not fearing 'the terror of night, nor the arrow that flies by day'. He found it perfect pre-match reading for the combative matches he took part in.

MESSI'S MEDITATION

Lionel Messi was born in Santa Fe, Argentina, in 1987. He joined Barcelona in 2000 and quickly became one of the world's most respected footballers. He has won the La Liga six times. The forward has also starred on the world stage with Argentina.

SILENCE IS GOLDEN FOR LIONEL

Some footballers psyche themselves up for a game by blasting loud music into the dressing room, or engaging in epic bouts of noisy 'banter' with their teammates. Dressing rooms are also known to reverberate with the gladiatorial cries of motivational managers. However, for Lionel Messi of Barcelona, the serene and silent practice of meditation is the perfect pre-match tool. Officials at the Nou Camp say the Argentinian meditates before and after every game. Experts explain that meditation could bring a host of benefits to a footballer, including increased focus, endurance and spatial awareness. Having won numerous trophies, including personal honours such as the Fifa World Player of the Year award, Messi is one to emulate.

GRUBBING ON GRASS

Nicknamed the 'Mad Hatter', **Les Miles** began American football coaching back in the 1980s. He has been head coach at Oklahoma State and the LSU football team. He was born in Ohio in 1953.

HOW THE GREEN STUFF HUMBLED A COACH

American football coach Les Miles is one of
the game's true characters. His pre-game
ritual involved eating grass from the field.
He explained that this grazing moment
would 'humble' him 'as a man'. It reminded
him, he added, that he was 'part of the
field and part of the game'. He even took
to becoming something of a culinary critic,
comparing the taste of the grass at various
venues. 'You should have seen some
games before this. I can tell you one thing:
the grass in Tiger Stadium tastes best.' At
other venues he would sometimes criticize
the quality of the turf, describing it as
'undergrown' or 'not full-bodied'.

MINOSO'S SHOWER

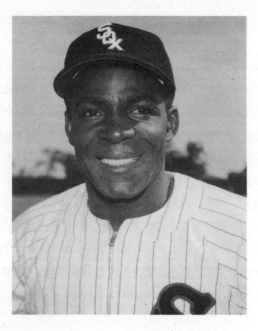

Minnie Minoso was a White Sox great who spent thirteen full seasons in the major baseball leagues between 1949 and 1980. He was elected into the Chicago Sports Hall of Fame in 1984 and the World Baseball Hall of Fame in 1990. He was a trailblazer in the game: the first black player to appear for the White Sox and the first publicly acknowledged Cuban ball player in Major League Baseball.

ON A LOSING STREAK? BLAME YOUR CLOTHES . . .

When 1950s baseball star Minnie Minoso was enduring a hitless period for the White Sox, he decided that drastic action was needed. Minoso felt that his kit was to blame for this poor form, so he decided to jump into the shower while wearing it, to wash off the failure. This cleansing of his outfit seemed to do the trick – in the following game he was back to his best. His teammates were so impressed that they hopped into the shower wearing their own kits.

DOWN AT HEEL

One of the twentieth century's leading sex symbols, **Marilyn Monroe** was born in 1926. She started as a model in the 1940s, then in the '50s she became an internationally recognized actress and singer. She died in 1962.

HOW MARILYN PERFECTED HER WIGGLE

How did Marilyn Monroe always look so damned glamorous? This was for a host of reasons, of course, but one of her methods made her stand out – quite literally. Her hip-swinging walk was legendary, and it is widely believed that she pulled it off by shaving the heel of one shoe in each pair, so her walk would be quite naturally uneven. Indeed, some accounts say that she shaved as much as half an inch off one shoe in order to make the difference. This simple, homemade style technique was a footwear forerunner of the Croydon facelift – something democratically available to anyone who wanted to copy it.

BOBBY GETS CAUGHT SHORT

Bobby Moore OBE won 108 caps for the England team. His finest hour was as captain for England's victorious 1966 World Cup campaign. At club level Moore was captain of West Ham United for more than a decade.

MOORE FOOTBALL ECCENTRICITY

Bobby Moore is, at the time of writing, the only captain of the England national side to guide the team to victory in the World Cup. Yet even a figure as accomplished as this is not beyond embarrassing moments due to bizarre rituals. Moore insisted on being the final player in the changing room to put on his shorts. Sometimes, teammate Martin Peters would cheekily remove his shorts the moment he saw Moore don his. Moore would then remove his, only to replace them once Peters had put his own back on. He had to be last. Yet at the 1966 World Cup, both players came first.

LEFT BEFORE RIGHT

Alex Morgan is a leading American soccer player. She is an Olympic gold medallist and was named the 2012 female athlete of the year. At club level she has represented West Coast FC, Seattle Sounders Women and a host of other clubs.

BUT ALSO RIGHT BEFORE LEFT

United States women's football star Alex Morgan observes an elaborate string of rituals when she is getting into her kit before a game. She always rolls on her right sock before her left sock. Then, she puts on her left shoe before her right shoe and ties the laces on her left one first, before moving to the right to do the same. She has a number of other superstitions including never tucking in her shirt and only leaving the tiniest glimpse of shin guard showing above her socks. She was asked by *Outside* magazine why she followed this complicated tradition. 'There doesn't have to be a why,' she replied.

THE AUDACITY OF HOOPS

Born in 1961 in Hawaii, **Barack Obama** studied law at Harvard University and worked as a civil rights lawyer in Chicago. Between 1996 and 2004, he served in the Illinois state senate. He was then elected to the US Senate in 2004. He ran successfully for the White House in 2008 and 2012.

BARACK'S BELIEF IN BASKETBALL

Barack Obama has a longstanding tradition of playing basketball on election day. The habit began during the 2008 primaries. The presidential hopeful played basketball on the day of the Iowa caucus, and South Carolina primary, and won both votes. However, he did not play on the day of the New Hampshire primary, or the Nevada caucus, and lost both contests. Perceiving a connection, Obama played basketball on the days of both the 2008 and 2012 presidential elections. He was, of course, triumphant in both polls. As a spokesman explained, they felt they had made a mistake by not playing on the days of the votes they lost. 'We won't make that mistake again,' he said.

HOW UN-PEASANT

The son of Maximilian II and his wife, Marie of Prussia, **Otto of Bavaria** was king from 1886 to 1913. An eccentric man who in later life became known for his huge beard, he was reputed to suffer from mental illness. He died from a bowel obstruction in 1916.

KING OTTO'S TRIGGER-HAPPY RITUAL

Some people like to start their day with a cup of coffee. For others, dawn is all about a jog. Then there are those who swear by their morning swim. However, for King Otto of Bavaria, the best way to get the day under way was to shoot a peasant. In order to prevent his tyrannical habit from creating 365 casualties each year, his staff came up with a cunning plan. They would fill the king's gun with blank bullets, then one of them would dress as a peasant, playing dead when he fired at them. The trigger-happy monarch was fooled by the ruse and the peasants of the time were spared.

JOINING THE DOTS

Ann Patchett is best known for her 2001 novel *Bel Canto*, which won the Orange Prize for Fiction and the PEN/Faulkner Award. She has also written several other novels including *The Magician's Assistant* and *The Patron Saint of Liars*.

PATCHETT'S PENCHANT FOR PATHS PAST

The award-winning author Ann Patchett strongly believes that looking back can help propel you forward. She preaches that returning to a significant location of your past will help you understand the decisions you have made since you left there. During a speech at Sarah Lawrence College in 2006, she said: 'Coming back is the thing that enables you to see how all the dots in your life are connected, how one decision leads you to another, how one twist of fate, good or bad, brings you to a door that later takes you to another door, which aided by several detours – long hallways and unforeseen stairwells – eventually puts you in the place you are now.'

IT TAKES TWO, BABY

Named by *The Times* as one of the fifty greatest British writers since 1945, **Philip Pullman** is the author of the fantasy trilogy *His Dark Materials* and a fictionalized book about Jesus entitled *The Good Man Jesus and the Scoundrel Christ*. He was awarded a CBE in the New Year's Honours list in 2004.

YOU CAN FIND THE PERFECT BLEND

Philip Pullman has more writing rituals than you could shake a superstitious stick at. The celebrated author writes in a shed, using pen and paper – so far, so normal. However, Pullman insists on not tidying the shed during the writing of a book. He also insists on only using a ballpoint pen and narrow-lined A4 paper 'with two holes, not four'. He writes to a strict target of three pages every day, approximately 1,100 words. Other habits he has had over the years include pausing to watch the Australian soap opera *Neighbours* – which he deems 'invaluable' – and always writing the first sentence of a fourth page, so he is never confronted with a blank page the next morning.

PEPE'S PETROL PATROL

Pepe Reina was born in Spain in 1982. At club level he has played for Barcelona, Villarreal, Liverpool and Napoli. He won the FA Cup during his years at Anfield, after starring in the penalty shoot-out.

WHY REINA FILLS UP ON MATCH DAY

'My desperation for success makes me superstitious,' says goalkeeper Pepe Reina. The Spaniard is not exaggerating when he describes himself as desperate. His pre-match rituals begin on the morning of each game. He drives to a particular petrol station and fills up his car. Most days he only needs to be at the pump for twenty seconds because his tank is already nearly full. Sometime Liverpool custodian Reina then goes in and hands over the tiny amount he owes to the baffled cashier. Once he arrives at the ground, he touches the turf, crosses himself and touches both posts. Then he walks four steps out into his six-yard area. This is elaborate pre-match preparation but it works for Pepe.

WRITE AT NIGHT

US author **Anne Rice** has written works in a number of genres including Gothic fiction, Christian literature and erotica. She is best known for her series *The Vampire Chronicles*. She was born in New Orleans in 1941.

THE VAMPIRE AUTHOR SLEPT BY DAY

When Anne Rice wrote her novel *Interview with the Vampire* she lived more as a bat than a vampire, writing by night and sleeping during the day. 'I just found it the time when I could concentrate and think the best,' she said. 'I needed to be alone in the still of the night, without the phone, without friends calling, with my husband sound asleep. I needed that utter freedom.' More recently she has found daytime writing more effective, though she has thrown in some new rituals to the mix. These include drinking copious quantities of Diet Coke on ice. Overall, she has concluded, it is important to have routines but also to be flexible enough to change and update them.

SWING, PRESS AND TOUCH

Stephanie Rice came to international prominence when she won the 200- and 400-metre individual medley titles at the Beijing 2008 Olympics. She has been voted Australia's most popular Olympic athlete and been awarded the Medal of the Order of Australia.

AN AUSSIE SWIMMER'S WARM-UP

If there were gold medals handed out for superstitious behaviour, Stephanie Rice would fancy her chances for the place on the top of the podium. However, getting the Australian swimmer up there might be a time-consuming project. For Rice goes through what can only be described as a complex pre-swim routine. She does eight arm swings, four goggle presses and four cap touches. 'It looks really weird,' she concedes of her ritual, 'but it's so comfortable to me it comes as second nature now.' Speaking to CNN, she added: 'I believe truly in superstition and karma, and everything happens for a reason.'

THE BULLET SPRINTER

Sanya Richards-Ross won the gold medal in the 4x400-metre relay at three successive Olympic Games tournaments: 2004, 2008 and 2012. She has also been world champion in the 400 metres. Born in 1985, she began running as a seven-year-old.

SANYA'S LUCKY NECKLACE

Olympic sprinter Sanya Richards-Ross was given a bullet necklace by her mother when she was in seventh grade. 'She told me I was faster than a speeding bullet and so I wear it to all of my competitions as kind of my good-luck charm,' the athlete told *Women's Running*. Richards-Ross wore it in every race bar one. The race in which she did not wear it, the highly successful runner finished only third, which added to her belief that it is vital for her to wear the bullet. She has also worn Chanel gold double-C earrings on the track. However, that seems to be more about looking good.

AS EASY AS 1, 4, 3 . . .

Frederick McFeely Rogers was an American broadcaster, author and songwriter. His most famous television show, which ran from the 1960s into the twenty-first century, was *Mister Rogers' Neighborhood*. It was a children's series, with light, if slightly earnest, content.

THERE WAS ONLY ONE WEIGHT FOR ROGERS

Fred Rogers lived by a fairly settled daily routine. He would typically wake at 5.30 a.m. and go to bed at 9.30 p.m. Early to bed, early to rise. He loved to swim, read, write and pray. Most days he would treat himself to a late-afternoon nap, too. However, he did have one peculiar ritual for life. When he weighed himself one day, he noticed that his weight was 143 pounds and realized that the three figures in that number are equivalent to the number of letters in each word of the phrase: I love you. In that moment, he decided it was important to maintain that precise weight at all times. According to reports, he managed to do just that. Lovely.

MITT'S TRIBUTE TO DAD

Born in 1947, **Mitt Romney** is an American politician and businessman. He served as the Governor of Massachusetts between 2003 and 2007, before running as a Republican in the 2012 US presidential election. He was the first Mormon to be a major-party presidential nominee.

HOW ROMNEY PREPARES FOR DEBATES

US Republican politicians may not often wear their gentler side on their sleeve but Mitt Romney's big secret is that he is a bit of a softie at heart. His wife, Ann, revealed that immediately before any major political debate he follows the same ritual. 'As soon as he gets on stage . . . he takes off his watch and puts it on the podium . . . then he writes "Dad" on the piece of paper,' she told CNN. 'And that's amazing, because he loves his dad, respects his dad. Doesn't want to do anything that would not make his father proud . . . I love the fact that Mitt does that. So he writes that.'

THE TERROR OF 13

Franklin D. Roosevelt was the thirty-second
President of the United States. He served for
twelve years, from 1933 to 1945, the only president
ever to serve more than eight years. He built the
New Deal coalition.

WHY FDR PREFERRED 14

Triskaidekaphobia is a glorious word.
It means a fear of the number 13 – and
avoiding that number is a ritual that
Franklin D. Roosevelt swore by. The
American president would reschedule
flights to avoid ones that fell on a date or
time including the dreaded figure. If he
realized his dining party would include
thirteen guests, he would invite his
secretary to join them. Napoleon had the
same phobia and would refuse to dine in
parties of thirteen. Triskaidekaphobia has
actually been a widespread concern in
France, particularly during the eighteenth
and nineteenth centuries.

THE SHRINKING SAINT

Patrick Roy played for the Montreal Canadiens and the Colorado Avalanche. He won two Stanley Cups with each outfit. He was inducted into the Hockey Hall of Fame in 2006. He has since coached.

HOW TO SHRINK THE GOAL

Patrick Roy was one of the finest ice-
hockey goaltenders in the history of the
NHL. The former Montreal Canadien ace
believed that a key part of his success
was a pre-match ritual. He would skate
backwards towards the goal then turn to
face it at the last moment. He believed
that this made the goal he would be
tending reduce in size. Roy was also one
to chat with the goalposts during the
game, thanking them if they deflected a
puck. He would even caress them at times.
Such was his behaviour that he became
nicknamed Saint Patrick.

OH, YOU ROTTEN THING

Johann Christoph Friedrich von Schiller
was a leading German dramatist, historian and
poet. He was also a philosopher. Schiller, who
lived from 1759 to 1805, wrote several influential
works on aesthetics.

RANCID APPLES AS WRITING FUEL

An apple a day keeps the doctor away, they say. However, for poet Friedrich Schiller, they also kept writer's block away. He stuffed one of his desk drawers full of decaying apples in order to motivate himself to crack on with his writing. He found that their rancid, rotting smell was a great motivator. (There is no record of him doubling up the habit into a cider-making sideline. Nor is it known if he claimed the fruit as one of his five-a-day portions.) Another writing ritual of Schiller's, who also penned plays and essays, included working predominantly at night, with coffee or other refreshment by his side. However, it was that rotten fruit that really spurred him on.

LOOK BACK TO MOVE FORWARD

Ariel Sharon was born in 1928 in the British
Mandate of Palestine. He was a decorated soldier
in the Israeli army, as a paratrooper, officer, then
revered field commander. He entered politics,
rising to serve as prime minister between 2001
and 2006. He died in 2014.

- - - - - - - - - - - - - - -

ARIEL'S REVERSE PSYCHOLOGY

Long before he became prime minister of the country, Ariel Sharon was a farmer in the state of Israel. The days were long, the fields on Shikim Farm were vast and the temperature was often painfully hot. It would have been very easy to give up. However, Sharon found that a simple technique, which his father had taught him when they sowed watermelon fields together, made the work much easier. Rather than looking ahead at the work he had left to do, he would look back at all the work he had already done. Sharon subsequently passed the tip down to his own children, the third generation of the family to enjoy its benefits.

HOW TO LIE WELL

Celebrated British poet and author **Dame Edith Sitwell** MBE (1887–1964) began publishing verse in 1913 and continued to do so at a prolific rate. Among her collections were *The Outcasts* and *Clowns' Houses*.

THE POET WHO LOVED HER BED

Edith Sitwell could more accurately have been named Edith Liewell. Like Truman Capote (page 42), the writer loved to write in bed. While it is widely believed that she used to lie in an open coffin for an hour before beginning work each day, some historians believe that is a myth. When a fellow poet was confronted with the theory, he responded bitterly: 'If only someone had thought to shut it!' As for her confirmed preference for writing in bed, Sitwell was enthusiastic. She said she loved to be able to write where and when she was 'sure of quiet'. She widely recommended more time in bed. 'All women should have a day a week in bed,' she believed.

THE MAGIC BRA

American cyclist **Evelyn Stevens** was born
in California in 1983 but was brought up in
Massachusetts. She quit working in finance in
2009 to compete in cycling full time. She quickly
made a success of it, and was the US national
time trial champion in 2010 and 2011.

STEVENS' SIBLING SUPERSTITION

Cyclist Evelyn Stevens keeps her good-luck charm very close to her heart. 'I have a lucky blue sports bra,' the professional road cyclist told an interviewer. 'My older sister gave it to me, and I did a few early races with it and started winning. Of course, it wasn't the training or my ability, it was the blue lucky sports bra.' Stevens, who competed at the London 2012 Olympics, has worn the bra in nearly all the bike races she has competed in. The former banker says she is often asked if she washes it and she assures everyone that she does indeed do that.

SHORT AND QUIRKIES

Jason Terry is a celebrated American basketball player who plays shooting guard. His nickname, Jet, comes from his initials, as his middle name is Eugene.

THE BASKETBALL PLAYER WHO SWAPS SIDES

Jason Terry has a strange ritual for the night before a match – he wears replica shorts of the opponents' kit. He started doing so while at college, though originally he would wear his own team's kit. However, he began to feel bored of his own kit and started to wear the opposition's instead. While this is his central, and most idiosyncratic, ritual, Terry is a man with many superstitions. He also eats chicken before every game, wears high socks on court, and changes his footwear if a game is not going well. 'I'm a different dude,' Terry told the *New York Times*. 'My daughters say I'm a weirdo.'

VERY SUPERSTITIOUS

John Terry has made over five hundred appearances for Chelsea, many as captain, and has also captained the English national side. He has led Chelsea to a host of trophies including Premier League titles, FA cups and the UEFA Champions League.

JOHN'S ENDLESS RITUALS AND CHARMS

John Terry was once asked whether he is superstitious and whether he has any rituals. 'I have about fifty,' he replied. Among this list of charms, traditions and rituals are sitting on the same seat on the team bus, parking in the same spot in the car park and listening to the same CD (an Usher album) before each match. The Chelsea and England defender has also worn the same lucky pair of shin pads for the past ten years. He ties the tapes around his socks exactly three times. On one occasion his lucky car-park spot was taken. He spent two hours arranging for the offending vehicle to be moved.

STAYING AWAKE

Best known for his contributions to the field of electricity, **Nikola Tesla** was a Serbian-American inventor who lived from 1856 to 1943. His stamina and enthusiasm were legendary; it is said that he once worked in a laboratory for eighty-four hours without any rest or sleep.

HOW TO BE AN ICONIC INSOMNIAC

The inventor Nikola Tesla gave sleep short shrift – quite literally. He followed a similar sleep pattern to Leonardo da Vinci (page 184) but took it to new extremes. He claimed he never slept for more than two hours each day, as he felt that getting as many waking hours into each twenty-four-hour period as possible was the route to success. For Tesla, there was no 'thrill' life could offer that bettered the feeling in the 'human heart' of the inventor when they saw a project through to fruition. 'Such emotions make a man forget food, sleep, friends, love, everything,' he said.

WOOD YOU BELIEVE IT?

Benicio del Toro's best-known roles came in the movies *Traffic* and *The Usual Suspects*. The Puerto Rican actor and producer has also appeared in other movies including *Fear and Loathing in Las Vegas*, and television series such as *Miami Vice*.

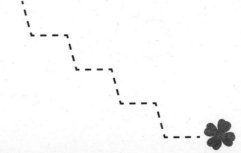

BENICIO'S LUCKY RING

The 'touch wood' superstition is one of the most familiar and widespread luck traditions known to man. However, what do you do if you want to follow it, and there is no wood immediately to hand? Actor Benicio del Toro can help us. When he was nominated for an Oscar in the Best Supporting Actor category for *Traffic*, he spoke about a lucky charm he wore on his finger. It was a ring with a wooden, rather than stone, centre. 'What I like is that I can knock on wood any time,' he explained. But did it work, you ask. Yes, his touching wood did the trick – he won the gong.

MARKING TWAIN'S WORDS

Mark Twain, who was born Samuel Langhorne Clemens in 1835, wrote *The Adventures of Tom Sawyer* and *The Adventures of Huckleberry Finn*. Both works became hugely influential. Twain is considered one of the finest American authors of all time.

HOW TO WRITE THROUGH A STORM

Mark Twain was far from a fair-weather writer: there was little that could stop him writing once he got going. He worked in a small, private study and on hot days he would throw open the doors and windows and carry on writing. He would also continue writing, he said, 'in the midst of a hurricane', by anchoring his papers down with weights. If any of his loved ones wanted to capture his attention, they would blow a loud horn they had acquired. Once he finally finished in the evening, he would read his day's work to his family. While he was a dedicated worker, Twain was a poor sleeper. To overcome his bedroom insomnia, he took to sleeping on the bathroom floor.

ROCKY RACCOON

Steven Tyler's screaming vocals on Aerosmith's songs are one of the most distinctive motifs in rock. The high-energy frontman has also judged on *American Idol*, written a memoir and made guest appearances with other acts.

THE TOOTH ABOUT TYLER'S PENDANT

Steven Tyler is a man draped in accessories. He dons elaborate scarves, plentiful jewels and even birds' feathers. Among all these items is one he wears less for its visual impact and more for the good fortune he believes it brings him. It is a necklace formed from the four teeth of a raccoon he caught when he was just a little lad. 'I wear it for good luck,' he told *Parade* magazine. The Aerosmith frontman is quite the fan of raccoons: he had one as a pet when he was a kid and carried it around draped over his shoulder.

COUNTRY AND COOKIES

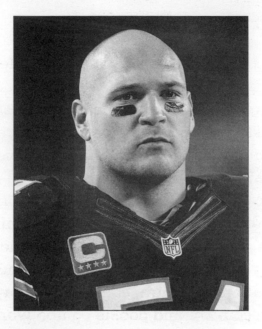

Brian Urlacher spent all of his thirteen-year career with the Chicago Bears. Born in 1978, he began in college football with the University of New Mexico. He won several personal awards with the Bears.

HOW BRIAN THE BEAR PSYCHED UP

Brian Urlacher was a fearsome and feared American football linebacker for the Chicago Bears. One of the NFL's most respected defensive players, he made for a formidable figure on the field. However, his ritual of preparation was not quite as thunderous as one might imagine. Urlacher liked to prepare for the fray by listening to the sweet strains of country music and eating chocolate chip cookies. He had a reputation for tough, competitive playing, so the country and cookie combo worked for him.

THAT'S A NAP, FOLKS!

One of the finest creative minds of the Italian
Renaissance, **Leonardo da Vinci** lived an
extraordinary life as an artist, sculptor, scientist
and inventor. He died in 1519, at the age of sixty-
seven, having epitomized the humanist ideal.

THE SHUT-EYE CODE DA VINCI LIVED BY

When it came to sleeping, the legendary
Leonardo da Vinci followed a principle of
'little, but often'. He would take a twenty-
minute nap every four hours. This sleeping
pattern is a polyphasic cycle known as the
'Uberman sleep schedule'. If that sounds
a little jargony to you, it can also be called
power-napping. Modern-day scientists
have mixed feelings over da Vinci's habit.
They point out that it gave him more
waking hours per day than most people,
but also that it deprived him of the full
ninety-minute cycle of phases required for
a healthy body and mind. Still, as da Vinci's
curriculum vitae shows, the artist and
inventor didn't do so badly in life.

THE NAKED TRUTH

Born François-Marie Arouet, the writer known better as **Voltaire** lived from 1694 to 1778. A versatile and punchy writer, historian and philosopher, he wrote more than two thousand books and pamphlets.

VOLTAIRE'S CURIOUS WRITING DESK

Voltaire preferred a rather full-on working day. The French enlightenment scribe would frequently remain in bed until midday, having spent the morning reading and dictating passages of writing to one of his staff. Despite rising around lunchtime he would not actually eat a midday meal as such, instead getting by on coffee and chocolate. He worked throughout the afternoon and would sometimes put even more working time in after dinner. A friend commented that the prolific Voltaire would work up to twenty hours each day. However, the most curious of his writing rituals was that he would, reportedly, sometimes use the naked back of his lover as a writing desk.

TURK A LOOK AT THIS LOT

A right-handed relief pitcher, **Steven John 'Turk' Wendell** played for the Pulaski Braves, Chicago Cubs, New York Mets, Philadelphia Phillies and Colorado Rockies. Born in 1967, his career ran from 1993 to 2004.

WENDELL AND HIS WONDERFUL QUIRKS

Turk Wendell was quite a character. He took the concept of superstition to dizzy new heights during his eleven-year baseball career. He would always jump over the baselines on the field. Between innings, he would brush his teeth, but while he was pitching he would chew black licorice. Around his neck he strung a necklace, bearing the teeth of wild animals he had successfully hunted. During contractual negotiations with the New York Mets in 2000, he requested that his fee be $9,999,999.99. The reason he was willing to surrender a cent? His uniform number was 99, and he wanted his contract to match.

WEST HITS THE 'REPEAT' BUTTON

Born in the 1930s, **Paul West** is the author
of poems, essays, memoirs and over twenty
novels. He has won many honours, including
the American Academy of Arts and Letters
Literature Award.

THE AUTHOR AND HIS SONATINA

Sometimes a piece of music just gets anchored to a particular emotion in your mind. We all have a song that reminds us of a particularly sad or happy time. For some artistic people, a song can become linked to the creative process. Take Paul West. While the author and poet wrote his book *The Place in Flowers Where Pollen Rests*, he listened non-stop to one piece of music. He chose a sonatina by the Italian composer Ferruccio Busoni to listen to as he wrote the novel on his typewriter. Over and over West played the music and only when he had finished writing his story, which is set in North Arizona, did he allow himself respite from its strains.

THE BAR OF IDEAS

Born in 1951, **Kate White** is an American editor, writer and speaker. She was editor-in-chief of *Cosmopolitan* between 1998 and 2012 and is the author of eight novels, as well as several non-fiction titles.

TURNING YOUR KITCHEN INTO A NIGHT-TIME WRITING PUB

Magazine editor Kate White found that the best way to write was to stand up in her kitchen and imagine she was running a pub. Describing the habit as her 'craziest trick', she explained that she would down a couple of espresso coffees, switch on the television, then work standing at the rolling butcher-block counter in her kitchen. 'If I were to work sitting down, I'd fall asleep,' she told *Fast Company*. 'I know it sounds awful, but I think of it as if I'm tending bar in the evening – a bar of ideas,' added the former editor-in-chief of *Cosmo*. Having the television on in the background ensured she never felt lonely.

CHECK THE BOUNCES

Serena Williams frequently holds top spot in the women's tennis ranking. She has won numerous titles including the French Open, US Open, WTA Tour Championships and Olympic ladies singles champion. She is the only female player to have won over $50 million in prize money.

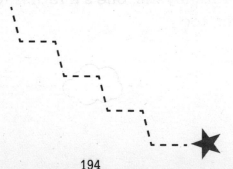

SERENA'S SASSY SUPERSTITIONS

Serena Williams has enough superstitions to fill a tennis bag. A key habit of the three-time Wimbledon champion is to bounce the ball five times before her first serve, then twice before her second serve. She also carries her shower sandals to the court with her and ties her training shoelaces a particular, though unspecified, way. If she builds up a good run during a tournament she will continue to wear the same pair of socks for as long as it goes on. Even in the superstitious world of tennis, with its plentiful eccentric characters and memorable habits, Williams qualifies as a first-rate mystic. She's a rather talented player, too.

HURL AN OCTOPUS

The Detroit Red Wings is a professional ice hockey team that was founded in 1926. It was originally known as the Detroit Cougars. They are one of the original six teams of the National Hockey League.

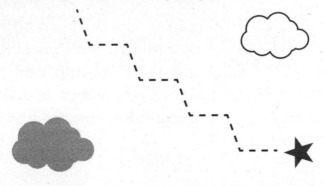

WHY WINGS FANS TOSS EIGHT-LEGGED CREATURES

During an NHL game involving the Detroit Red Wings in 1952, a fan threw a dead octopus on to the ice. It was interpreted as a symbolic, if slightly unsightly, act: the eight legs of the octopus representing the eight wins the team needed to secure the Stanley Cup. The Red Wings won the tie and thus was a peculiar tradition born. It became known as the 'Legend of the Octopus'.
It continues to this day: during one game, fans threw thirty-six octopuses, and the team's unofficial mascot is a purple octopus named Al. The club management has since refined the rules over the throwing, and subsequent clearing, of octopuses. In 2008 a controversy over these rules became known as 'Octopus-gate'.

A HELPING HAND

A leading American novelist of the early twentieth century, **Thomas Wolfe** penned such works as *Look Homeward, Angel* and *The Lost Boy*. Even after his death he continued to inspire, with the 'beat' writers citing him as an influence.

THE CATCHY CARESS OF (JOHN) THOMAS

Thomas Wolfe found that playing with himself was a good way of getting his creative juices flowing. It all started one evening in 1930, as he suffered from writer's block. Wolfe gave up for the night and stripped naked as he prepared to go to bed. However, as he peered out of the window, he felt inspired again. He returned to his desk and wrote through the night. He put this sudden inspiration down to the fact he had been playing with his private parts by the window. This had given him a 'good male feeling', he said. So whenever he found himself short of creative spark, he would once more plough his 'male configurations' until inspiration returned.

THE RED EYE OF THE TIGER

One of the most successful players in the history of golf, **Tiger Woods** won his first major in 1997, in the form of the Masters. He has since won fourteen major professional championships and been awarded PGA Player of the Year a record eleven times.

WOODS SALUTES SCARLET SHIRTS

Why does Tiger Woods always wear red on Sundays during golf competitions? Lots of viewers and fans have noted that he appears in the colour during big tournaments. This is more than mere coincidence. The champion explains that it is a tradition that began in his junior golf days. 'I just stuck with it out of superstition, and it worked,' he told the Golf Channel. 'I just happened to choose a school [whose uniform] was red, and we wore red on our final day of events. So it worked out.' He intends to maintain this superstitious habit for some time to come. 'I've had a few wins wearing red, and it's not going to change,' he said.

BEAT YOURSELF UP

John Lloyd Young is a critically acclaimed, award-winning actor. He starred as Frankie Valli in Broadway's production of *Jersey Boys*. He has also been appointed by Barack Obama to a presidential committee on arts and humanities.

THE JERSEY BOY WHO TAKES HIMSELF ON

As *Jersey Boys* actor John Lloyd Young waits backstage before each evening performance, the Broadway star goes through a number of rituals. Some of these are fairly mainstream and predictable: for instance, the Tony Award winner inhales steam, stretches his muscles and undergoes a forty-minute vocal warm-up. Then, it gets a little weird. He pulls his tongue using a paper towel and beats himself with rubber massage mallets. 'How very Catholic,' he comments of the two oddball habits. Indeed. Next to those, his favourite pre-show meal of chicken parmesan panini seems very tame – though 'fish on Friday' would have at least continued the Catholic theme of his activities each time he prepares to put in another show-stealing performance.

ZARDARI GOT THEIR GOAT

Asif Ali Zardari served as the eleventh president of Pakistan between 2008 and 2013. He rose to prominence after marrying Benazir Bhutto in 1987, becoming her 'First Gentleman'. He spent several years in jail on corruption charges.

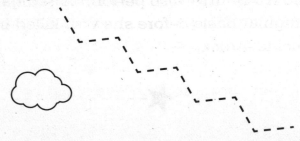

HOW TO WARD OFF EVIL EYE

Pakistan president Asif Ali Zardari preferred to slaughter goats than peasants – unlike King Otto (see page 140). Zardari is said to have slaughtered a black goat each day at his Islamabad home. He reportedly believed that this ritual would repel 'evil eyes' and protect him against 'black magic'. His spokesman confirmed that the president would slaughter goats under a ritual called *sadiqa*. As part of that ritual, the meat of the goat would then be distributed to the poor and starving. A spokesman confirmed he had seen it happen 'quite often' but 'not exactly every day'. Zardari's wife, the late Benazir Bhutto, also performed *sadiqa* on a regular basis before she was killed in a suicide attack.

ICE, ICE, BABY . . .

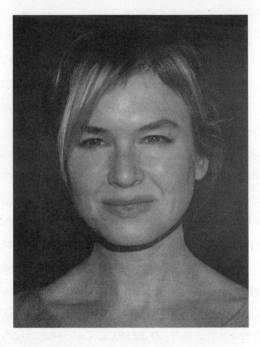

US actress **Renée Zellweger** first came to widespread attention in the mid-1990s for her role in *Jerry Maguire*. Yet it was her lead role in the Bridget Jones movies that made her internationally renowned. She has since won an Academy Award for *Cold Mountain*.

RENÉE'S FREEZING FOOD FAD

When in character as the much-loved Bridget Jones, Renée Zellweger worried about calories and attempted, with varying degrees of success, to diet. However, the actress herself has an eating ritual which she sticks by through, well, thick and thin. Throughout each day, Zellweger snacks on ice cubes. She says this helps her feel full and fresh, and therefore ready to take on the challenges a day can bring. 'As long as I get that "constant feed" feeling, it's semi-tolerable,' said Zellweger. She has also been known to snack on bamboo and to walk long distances to meetings, to shed pounds and focus her mind. 'V. good', as Bridget Jones would note.

ABOUT THE AUTHOR

Chas Newkey-Burden is a journalist, columnist and author. His books include *Simon Cowell: The Unauthorised Biography, Help! I'm Turning Into My Dad,* and *The All-New Official Arsenal Miscellany.* He also co-wrote, with Julie Burchill, *Not In My Name: A Compendium of Modern Hypocrisy.* Follow him on **Twitter:** @AllThatChas

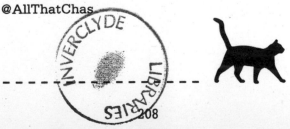